Preparing Written Assignments

Contents

LESSON 1	Planning Your Homework	2
LESSON 2	Following Written Directions	4
LESSON 3	Organizing Before Writing	6
LESSON 4	Preparing Neat, Well-Organized Papers	8
LESSON 5	Proofreading Your Assignments	10
LESSON 6	Advance Planning for Large Written Assignments	14
LESSON 7	Choosing a Topic	16
LESSON 8	Taking Notes When Gathering Information	18
LESSON 9	Organizing Information	22
LESSON 10	Writing a First Draft	24
LESSON 11	Writing the Final Copy	26
LESSON 12	Making Your Writing Come Alive	28
REVIEW	Preparing Written Assignments	30
REVIEW	Preparing Large Written Assignments	31
ANSWER KEY		Inside Back Cover

Acknolwedgments

Executive Editor: Diane Sharpe
Supervising Editor: Stephanie Muller
Design Manager: Laura Cole
Cover Designer: D. Childress/Alan Klemp

Product Development: Curriculum Concepts, Inc.
Writer: Steven L. Stern

Illustrators: pp. 13, 15 Janet Bohn; pp. 22, 26 Pam Carroll; p. 20 Nancy Didion; pp. 3, 10, 28 Toby Gowing; p. 5 Al Hering; p. 6 Michael McDermott; pp. 17, 18 Lane Yerkes
Photography: cover © CE Nagele/FPG

ISBN 0-8114-2527-4

Copyright © 1994 Steck-Vaughn Company.
All rights reserved. No part of the material protected by this copyright may be reproduced or utilized in any form or by any means, electronic or mechanical, including photocopying, recording, or by any information storage and retrieval system, without permission in writing from the copyright owner. Requests for permission to make copies of any part of the work should be mailed to: Copyright Permissions, Steck-Vaughn Company, P.O. Box 26015, Austin, TX 78755. Printed in the United States of America.

1 2 3 4 5 6 7 8 9 0 CCG 00 99 98 97 96 95 94

Planning Your Homework

Planning ahead will help you complete your homework. Consider the assignments you have, how much time you have, and what books and other materials you will need.

Ask Yourself

Which of these statements describe your work habits? Write <u>yes</u> or <u>no</u>.

1. I put off doing things until the last minute. _____

2. At home, I often can't find the materials I need to do my work. _____

3. I don't have enough time to get all my homework done. _____

4. I leave books and papers at school that I need to do my homework. _____

5. I often say, "I'll do that tomorrow," but then I don't. _____

If you wrote <u>yes</u> for any statement, you need to improve your planning!

Plan Ahead for Homework

- Be sure to write homework assignments and their due dates correctly onto your assignment calendar or into your assignment book.
- Review assignments before leaving school. If you are not sure you understand an assignment, ask your teacher.
- Think ahead. Estimate how much time you will need for each assignment. To be safe, leave yourself extra time.
- Plan when you will do your assignments and in what order. Remember to allow time for chores and after-school activities.
- Divide large assignments into smaller tasks. For example, take notes for a writing assignment one day. Use those notes to outline the assignment the next day. Then write the assignment the day after.
- Work in a quiet, well-lighted place where you won't be disturbed.
- Before you begin work, gather the books and materials you will need.

Try It Out

Suggest a solution for each problem described below. For hints, look at the **How To** box.

1. **PROBLEM:** When Vicki gets home from school, she relaxes until dinner time. After dinner, she takes a shower. She usually starts her homework at 7:30. In order to complete all her assignments, Vicki often has to stay up very late.

   SOLUTION: _____
   _____

2. **PROBLEM:** Robert likes to do his homework in the kitchen. Each time the kitchen phone rings, he jumps up to answer it. Sometimes the call is for him. Other times, it's for his mother or sister. Because of all the phone interruptions, Robert's homework often takes him twice as long as it should.

   SOLUTION: _____
   _____

3. **PROBLEM:** Christine's teacher announces on Monday that there will be a math test Friday. Christine always studies for tests the night before. This time, she's worried. There's so much to study, she's not sure she can do it all Thursday night. What's worse, there's one type of problem she doesn't completely understand.

   SOLUTION: _____
   _____

What Have I Learned?

How can the **How To** suggestions help you plan ahead on Wednesday for a complicated assignment that is due the following Tuesday?

_____
_____
_____
_____

Following Written Directions

LESSON 2

Directions tell you what to do and often give clues that tell how to do it. Read directions carefully and completely before you begin to write.

Ask Yourself

The questions, problems, and activities in schoolbooks begin with written directions. How important do you think these directions are? Read each statement below. If you think the statement is true, write true next to it. If you think it is not true, write false.

1. Reading directions more than once is a waste of time. _____

2. Only the first sentence in a set of directions really matters. _____

3. Following directions is important for math but not for social studies. _____

4. A good way to save time is to skim directions and get right to work. _____

5. By age ten or eleven, students know enough to be able to skip directions. _____

If you thought any of the statements were true, think again. They are all false.

How To

Follow Written Directions

- Always take time to read directions carefully at least once before you begin work. Read every word!
- Watch for key words that tell you what to do, especially verbs, such as *read*, *write*, *circle*, *underline*, *choose*, *use*, *compare*, *estimate*, and *explain*.
- Watch for sentences that provide clues or extra information to help you complete the assignment.
- Think carefully about questions. Ask yourself exactly what information your answer must contain.
- If you are not sure what a word means, look it up in a dictionary.
- If you are confused about directions, ask for help.

Try It Out

Read each set of directions. Then answer the questions that follow.

A. Solve by finding the pattern. Write the rule. Then write the next two numbers in the pattern.

39, 32, 25, . . .

1. What key words tell you what to do? _____
2. What two pieces of information are you asked for? _____
_____

B. Write a paragraph explaining why people do not see a full moon every night. Draw pictures to make your explanation clear.

1. What key words tell you what to do? _____
2. What two tasks are you asked to do? _____
_____

C. Sometimes people laugh to keep from crying. How do you think Helen really feels about her lost dog? Give examples from the story to support your opinion. Write complete sentences.

1. What key words tell you what to do? _____
2. What information must your answer contain? _____
_____
3. Which sentence provides a clue to help you answer the question? _____
_____

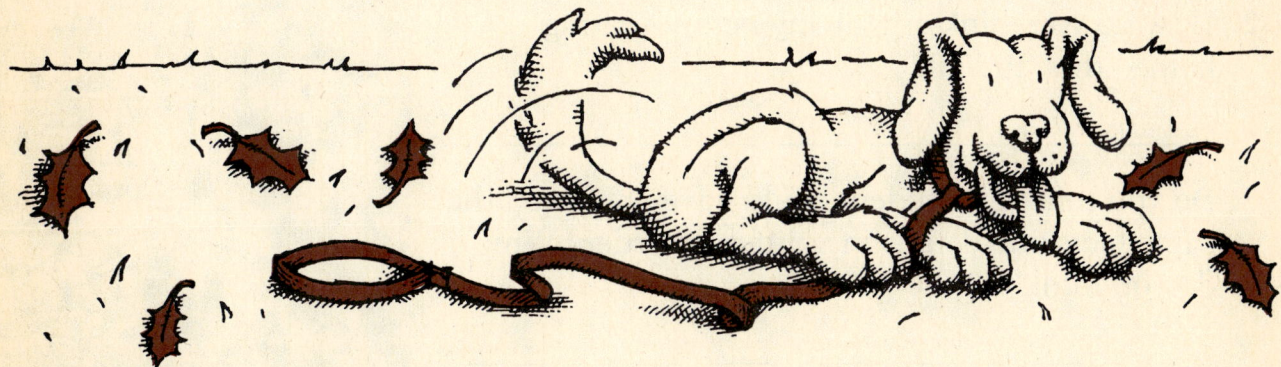

What Have I Learned?

Look back at the first two statements in *Ask Yourself*. On a separate sheet of paper, explain why each of these two statements is false.

LESSON 3
Organizing Before Writing

Before you write, organize your thoughts. Decide what ideas you will include and in what order you will present them. This will make your assignments easier to write.

Ask Yourself

Shown below is the plan a student made for writing a social studies assignment. It is followed by a paragraph the student wrote afterward. Read the plan and the paragraph. Then answer the questions.

My main idea: Very little grows in the desert.
Facts or details about my main idea:
sand surface – rocky – little rainfall – only cactuses grow

Deserts are dry areas where few plants will grow. Many deserts have a surface of sand. Others are rocky. Deserts have so little rainfall that only cactuses and a small number of other plants can survive there.

1. A **topic sentence** states the main idea. What is the topic sentence of the paragraph?
   _____
   _____

2. How do you think organizing before writing helped this student?
   _____

3. Do you think the student could have presented the same facts and details in a different order? Why do you think so?
   _____
   _____

Do you always make a plan before you start to write?

6

How To

Organize Before Writing

- Think about your writing purpose. For example, are you answering a question? Writing a summary? Stating your opinion?
- Decide what the main idea is.
- Choose facts or details to support or develop the main idea.
- List the main idea. Then list the supporting facts or details in the order you plan to use them.
- If you are writing more than one paragraph, decide in what order you will present your ideas, and plan each paragraph.

Try It Out

Suppose that your teacher gave you the homework assignment described below. To organize your thoughts for the assignment, answer the following questions.

Write a paragraph describing your favorite room in your home. Include facts or details that help show why the room is your favorite.

1. What would be your main idea?
   _____

2. List three facts or details that you would use to support or develop your idea. Number them in the order you would use them.
   _____
   _____
   _____

3. What would the topic sentence for the paragraph be?
   _____
   _____

What Have I Learned?

Suppose your homework was to write a summary of a science experiment performed in class. On a separate sheet of paper, explain how you would use what you've learned in this lesson to organize your thoughts for the assignment.

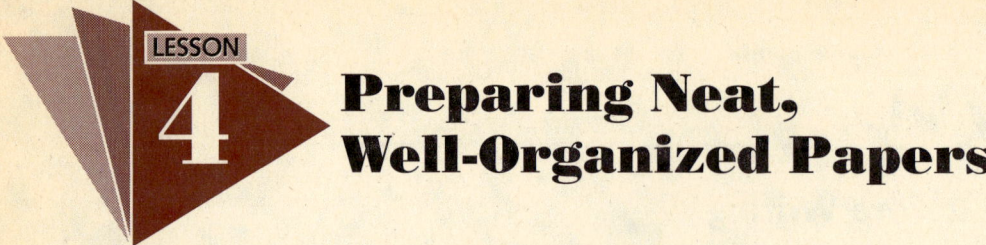

Preparing Neat, Well-Organized Papers

Neatness is an important habit to develop. Take pride in your work. Remember that neat, well-organized papers are easy to read, and they show that you're trying to do your best work.

Ask Yourself

Are your assignments neat and well organized? Read the following statements. Beside each one, write sometimes, always, or never.

1. My math papers look messy because of the way I erase. _____

2. My penmanship is easy to read. _____

3. I leave a neat right margin on my papers. _____

4. My written assignments have many words crossed out. _____

5. I leave information out of the heading. _____

6. I follow my teacher's directions for preparing papers. _____

Did you answer never for items 1, 4, and 5, and always for items 2, 3, and 6? If not, your papers may not be as neat as they should be.

How To

Prepare Neat, Well-Organized Papers

- Follow your teacher's directions.
- Choose an appropriate heading. Be sure it is clear and complete.
- Write neatly on the lines.
- Leave enough space between words to make your writing easy to read.
- Erase completely.
- Leave neat left and right margins.

Try It Out

A. Review the student's paper below. Then answer the questions.

```
Melinda          Math, page
Class 5-6H       February 21, 1994
1.  165.3    2.  80.07    3.   .89    4.  3.619    5.  54.90
   +128.9       -18.60       +.36       -2.320        +27.38
    294.2        61.47        1.25        1.299         82.28
```

1. Is the paper's heading complete? Explain your answer.

2. What suggestions can you make to improve this paper's neatness?

B. Review the following paper. Then answer the questions.

```
Nina Delgado                February
Science, page 203
   1. Clouds are collections of water droplets or ice crystals.
   2. Clouds form where water vapor in the air condenses or freezes.
      They form high in the air because it is colder there than at ground level.
   3. Cirrus clouds are thin and feathery. Cumulus clouds are big and
      puffy. Stratus clouds are flat and often dark.
```

1. Is the paper's heading complete? Explain your answer.

2. What suggestions can you make to improve this paper's neatness?

What Have I Learned?

Suppose you were a teacher. What three ways for preparing neat papers would you most want your class to use? Explain why. Use your own paper.

LESSON 5
Proofreading Your Assignments

Proofreading means checking over your work and correcting mistakes. It is important to take time to check and proofread written assignments before handing them in. Make corrections neatly. Rewrite sentences if necessary.

Ask Yourself

How important do you think proofreading is? Compare the paragraphs below. Then answer the questions.

BEFORE PROOFREADING

The ancient Egyptians had great mathmatical skill. They knew addition, subtraction multiplication, and division. They understood fractions they also new how to make exact measurments. Knowing mathematics helped helped the egyptians build the piramids.

AFTER PROOFREADING

The ancient Egyptians had great mathematical skill. They knew addition, subtraction, multiplication, and division. They understood fractions. They also knew how to make exact measurements. Knowing mathematics helped the Egyptians build the pyramids.

1. What spelling correction did the student make on the first line?

   _____

2. What punctuation did the student add on the second line?

   _____

3. What three changes did the student make on the fourth line?
_____

4. What change was made on the fifth line?
_____

5. What were the three changes made on the last line?
_____
_____

Do you see the difference proofreading your work can make?

How To

Proofread Your Assignments

After you finish an assignment, reread it to make sure it is complete and correct. Use this checklist and the proofreader's marks on page 12 when proofreading.
- Did I answer all of the assigned questions?
- Have I checked all my answers and double-checked facts, dates, and numbers?
- Did I express my ideas clearly?
- Did I include facts or details to support my ideas?
- Do all the words and sentences make sense?
- Do my sentences begin with a capital letter and end with the correct punctuation mark?
- Did I capitalize proper nouns?
- Did I use commas, quotation marks, and apostrophes correctly?
- Did I indent paragraphs?
- Did I check the spelling of difficult words in a dictionary?
- Did I use the proper heading?

Try It Out

A. The statements on the following page are sample homework answers. Each answer contains two errors. Proofread the answers. Neatly correct the errors. Look at the **How To** box and the proofreader's marks for help.

11

Proofreader's Marks

~~but~~ e	Cross this word out.
b^r^ave	Add this letter or word.
for / ~~four~~	Change this word.
m̲e̲	Make this a capital letter.
T̸he	Make this a lower-case letter.
¶ He is	Begin a new paragraph.
end ⊙	Add a period.
happy‸but	Add a comma.
‿was‿	Change this word order.

1. The main character of the story is daniel. He is a true hero because he never gives up

2. Zero multiplied by any number zero. For example, 0 × 9 = 9.

3. The part of the atlantic Ocean between Central and south America is the Caribbean Sea.

4. trees, metals, and fossil fuels are examples of natural resources Water is a natural resource, too.

5. "Kilo" means 1,000. there are 1,00 meters in a kilometer.

6. Colombia exports most of it's coffee to other countrys.

B. Proofread the assignments. Make the needed changes and corrections. Note that a clue is given for each. Use the **How To** box for help.

1. **CLUE:** There are five errors in the paragraph.

   The machine I would like to invent is a robot vacuum cleaner It would have a built-in computer. You would have to push it around you're home only once. from then on, it would remember wear to go and what to clean. All you would have to do is turn it on.

12

2. **CLUE:** There are four errors in each paragraph.

> Asia is the largest continent in in the world. It's area is about 17 million square miles. The arctic Ocean is north of Asia, and the Indian Ocean is south To the east is the Pacific Ocean.
>
> Asia is a continent of many language. The greatest number of Asians speak Mandarin chinese. In India, the main language is Hindi. in other parts of Asia, people speak Japanese, Korean, and hundreds other languages.

3. **CLUE:** There are two errors in the first paragraph, four in the second.

> The word "phototropism" comes from the greek language. It means "turning toward the light."
>
> We demenstrated phototropism in a house plant. We put the plant on a windowsill each time we turned the pot, the plants leaves gradually moved so that they again faced the sun.

What Have I Learned?

1. How would you use the **How To** checklist to proofread math homework?

   _____
   _____
   _____

2. How would you use the **How To** checklist to proofread your answers to questions about something you have read?

   _____
   _____
   _____

13

Lesson 6: Advance Planning for Large Written Assignments

Some written assignments require several days. When you have a long or complicated assignment, begin by making a plan.

Ask Yourself

Can you recognize a good plan? Read the paragraph. Then answer the questions.

> The teacher announced that a book report was due in two weeks. Adam knew which book he wanted to read. However, he waited nine days to go to the library. When he finally got there, the book he wanted was checked out. He borrowed a different book, which was very long. By the time he finished reading it, he had only one day left to write the report.
>
> "It's not fair," Adam told Jenna. "We didn't get enough time."
>
> "I think you should have planned better," Jenna answered.

Who do you think was right, Adam or Jenna? Give reasons for your answer.

_____

_____

Do you use Adam's method to do large projects? If so, you need to plan better.

How To

Plan Ahead for Large Written Assignments

- In your assignment book or calendar, write exactly what the assignment is and when it is due.
- Think about the assignment. Do you understand it? If you have questions, ask your teacher.
- Make a plan. List the steps that you will follow to do the assignment.
- Estimate how long each step will take.
- Plan your time. Figure out when you will do each step.
- Build extra time into your schedule. Keep in mind that you will have other homework to do as well as after-school activities.
- Get the books or materials you will need. Don't wait until the last minute.

Try It Out

Make a step-by-step plan for each assignment. Next to each step, estimate how much time you would need to complete that step.

1. **ASSIGNMENT:** Write a one-page report explaining why leaves change color in the fall. Use at least one library book (other than an encyclopedia) to obtain your information.

   Due Date: one week from today

   My Plan and Time Estimate: _____
   _____
   _____
   _____

2. **ASSIGNMENT:** Ask a parent or relative to describe what his or her life was like when the person was your age. Prepare for the interview by making a list of ten questions you plan to ask. If you have a tape recorder, you may want to record your conversation.

   After the interview, write a report comparing the person's life to your own. In what ways was it different? How was it similar? Was the person's life harder or easier than yours is today? Why do you think so?

   Due Date: two weeks from today

   My Plan and Time Estimate: _____
   _____
   _____
   _____

What Have I Learned?

Suppose your teacher gave you the interview assignment above. On a sheet of paper, make a calendar for the next two weeks. Decide when you would do each task in your plan. Remember to allow yourself time for other homework and after-school and weekend activities.

Lesson 7: Choosing a Topic

A written assignment takes time and effort. To make the task easier and more enjoyable, choose your topic wisely. When choosing the topic for a written assignment, pick one that truly interests you or one that you feel strongly about. It is important to narrow the topic to make it as clear as possible.

Ask Yourself

Can you choose topics wisely? List two interesting topics for each assignment.

1. A paragraph expressing your opinion on a subject in the news: _____
_____
_____

2. A social studies report about a world problem: _____
_____
_____

3. A science report about an amazing discovery: _____
_____
_____

Which of these subjects would you rather do a written report on? Why?

How To

Choose a Topic

- List topics that you have strong feelings about. Then choose your favorite.
- Narrow the topic. For example, "Sports" is too broad a topic to cover in a report. "Team Sports" limits the topic, but not enough. "Baseball" is better, but still too general. "How Baseball Began in America" is clear and specific.
- Think ahead about how and where you will gather information. Be sure you will be able to find the facts you need in the time you have.

Try It Out

A. Each topic has been narrowed but is still too broad. Can you narrow it further?

1. Pollution ↦ Air Pollution ↦ _____

2. Cooking Is Fun ↦ Preparing a Meal ↦

   _____

3. Entertainment ↦ Video Games ↦

   _____

4. Civil Rights ↦ People Who Fought for

   Civil Rights ↦ _____

B. Two possible topics are given for each assignment below. Circle the one you think is better. Then explain your reasons. Check the **How To** box for hints.

1. For a composition:

   Why I Think People Under Age 18 Should Have the Right to Vote

   Voters and Voting

   _____

2. For a science report:

   What Causes Earthquakes?

   When Will the Next Earthquake Hit California?

   _____

3. For a newspaper or magazine article:

   The Person Who's Done the Most for Our Community

   People Who Live in the Neighborhood

   _____

What Have I Learned?

Complete the following statements.

1. When choosing a topic, the most important point to remember is

   _____

2. When choosing a topic, one thing you should never do is

   _____

17

Taking Notes When Gathering Information

To gather information for a report or other assignment, you often have to take notes. Find the information you need for your particular assignment. Then write down important points in your own words. Be sure your notes are correct.

Ask Yourself

Can you recognize good notes? Read the paragraph below. Then read the notes a student took to write a report on the topic "Pollution from Fossil Fuels." Answer the questions that follow.

> One of the major causes of pollution on our planet is the burning of fossil fuels. These fuels include oil, coal, and natural gas. They are used to generate electricity, to make metals out of ores, and to make chemicals. Fossil fuels are also used to heat homes, offices, and factories and to power vehicles. When the fuels are burned, waste products are released, polluting the air in a way that harms the earth's entire ecological system.

Pollution
- major causes
- fossil fuels
- waste
- fuel
- electricity

18

1. What is the main idea of the paragraph?
   _____
   _____

2. Do you think the student has written down the main idea clearly and completely? Explain your answer.
   _____
   _____

3. In writing down facts and details, what important information do you think the student has left out? Give at least three examples.
   _____
   _____

4. Suppose this student were writing a composition on the topic "Why Pollution Is Dangerous." Do you think this would be a useful paragraph to take notes on? Explain your answer.
   _____
   _____

How good are your note-taking skills? Read on for some tips on notetaking.

How To

Take Notes When Gathering Information

- Have a clear idea of your purpose for taking notes. For example, are you looking for details to describe a person or place? Or, are you looking for facts or examples to support an opinion?
- Keep your topic firmly in mind. Write down the main ideas and supporting facts and details that relate to your topic.
- Write words and phrases instead of whole sentences whenever you can.
- Use abbreviations and symbols for long or familiar words.
- Use your own words. If you must use someone else's words or if you copy words from a source, put them in quotation marks.
- Be sure your notes are clear and easy to understand.
- Check to be sure you've written facts, numbers, and dates correctly.

19

Try It Out

A. Read the paragraph. Then fill in the lines as though you were taking notes.

Bats look quite different from one another. The largest are called fox bats. These bats are five feet across when their wings are spread. Compare them with the bumblebee bat. It weighs less than an ounce and is the world's smallest mammal.

1. Main idea of paragraph:
_____

2. Facts or details supporting that idea:
_____
_____
_____
_____

B. 1. Imagine you are writing a report on the topic "Gems: Nature's Treasures." Read each paragraph and take careful notes. Begin by determining the main idea of the paragraph. After you have finished taking notes, answer the questions that follow.

For thousands of years, people have valued precious stones because they are beautiful and rare. Gems have been used in bracelets, rings, and other kinds of jewelry. The most high-priced gem is the diamond. It is more special than other gems because of its hardness and clear brightness.

There are other precious stones besides the diamond. Emeralds, which are green, are almost as valuable as diamonds. A large, perfectly shaped emerald can be worth more than a smaller diamond. The ruby, the red gem, is next in value. It is not as hard as an emerald or a diamond. However, some people think rubies are more beautiful than any other gem. The sapphire is a blue gem. It is also rich in color, but it is not as rare as a ruby.

NOTES

_____
_____
_____
_____
_____
_____
_____
_____
_____

2. Suppose the topic of your report were "Diamonds: Nature's Greatest Treasure." Which of the notes that you took would you not have needed to write down?

_____
_____

3. Suppose you had to write a composition either agreeing or disagreeing with this statement: "Everyone loves diamonds." What information in the paragraphs might you use in your composition?

_____
_____

What Have I Learned?

Suppose a friend asked you for the most important dos and don'ts of good notetaking. Write what you think are the three most important dos and the three most important don'ts. Write complete sentences.

DO	DON'T
_____	_____
_____	_____
_____	_____
_____	_____

21

Lesson 9: Organizing Information

Organizing information is an essential skill for preparing written assignments.

Ask Yourself

Read the three paragraphs below. Then answer the questions.

> A bird flies by flapping its wings. On the downstroke, the wings are forced down and back to push the bird upward and forward. On the upstroke, the wings are bent and the feathers are separated to let air through. This prevents the bird from being pushed down again. The tail is used for steering and slowing down.
>
> A bird needs strong muscles to fly. Its wings are moved by very large breast muscles. To make flying easier, a bird has light, hollow bones and a strong heart.
>
> Different birds have different types of wings. The type varies with the bird's method of flying. The albatross glides on long, thin wings. The hummingbird hovers on short, broad wings.

1. What is the main idea of each paragraph? (Look for the topic sentences.)

   _____
   _____
   _____

2. Could the writer have arranged the paragraphs in a different order? Give your reasons.

   _____
   _____

3. Do you think the writer developed each main idea with facts or details? Give an example.

   _____
   _____

Would it have been easy to answer questions 1 and 3 if the paragraphs had not been clearly arranged?

How To

Organize Information

- Think about the purpose of your assignment. For example, if you are comparing two books, will you write first about one book, then about the other? Or, will you first compare characters, then settings, and so on?
- Think about the length and structure of your assignment. For example, a long research report may have introductory and concluding paragraphs. A science report may have an "Observations" section.
- Decide what main ideas you will present. Each paragraph should have one main idea.
- Choose facts or details to support or develop each main idea.
- Arrange your main ideas and supporting facts or details in the order you plan to use them.

Try It Out

Imagine that your teacher gives you the following writing assignment:

Write a composition telling about a strange or funny experience you had. Describe the events in the order they happened. Tell when you had the experience, and describe your feelings at the time. Your paper should be at least three paragraphs long.

Organize the information you would use. Include main ideas and supporting details. Use the format below or another format that your teacher suggests. Use your own paper.

> **TOPIC:**
> Paragraph #1 main idea:
>   Supporting facts/details:
> Paragraph #2 main idea:
>   Supporting facts/details:
> And so on.

What Have I Learned?

Imagine that your assignment is to write a paper describing the life and accomplishments of someone you admire. On a separate sheet of paper, explain how you would use what you've learned in this lesson to do the assignment.

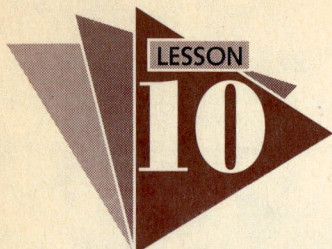

Writing a First Draft

When you have organized information and planned how to present it, you're ready to write a first draft. Remember that the first attempt at writing an assignment does not have to be perfect.

Ask Yourself

What steps are involved in writing a first draft? Below are the notes a student organized for a report and the first draft for its introductory paragraph. Read the notes and paragraph. Then answer the questions.

> TOPIC: Why Palm Trees Are Important
>
> Paragraph #1: introduction—the many uses of different types of palm trees
> - fruits, such as coconuts or dates for food
> - wood for furniture and housing
> - leaves for baskets and other items
> - oil for food and light
>
> Paragraph #2: kinds of food products from coconuts
> - milk   - oil

> People use the huge variety of palm trees for many purposes. They eat the fruits of different palms, such as coconuts or dates. They use the wood to make furniture and housing. The thick strong leaves are used to make such items as baskets. Palm oil is used in foods and is burned as a source of light.

1. What is the main idea of the paragraph? _____

2. Do you think this is a good opening paragraph for this report?

   Why or why not? _____

3. Could the student have arranged the details in a different order?

   Explain your answer. _____

4. Do you think the student's plan for the second paragraph is a good one?

   Why or why not? _____

How To

Write a First Draft

- Begin your first paragraph by writing the main idea. Usually, the first sentence will be your topic sentence.
- Next use the information you've gathered to write sentences that explain or tell more about the main idea.
- Write the following paragraphs in the same way. Start with a main idea. Then write sentences that develop the idea with facts and details.
- Try to make each paragraph flow smoothly into the next.
- Use your own words. <u>Never</u> copy word-for-word from a book unless you are including the information as a quote.
- Don't worry about spelling, capitalization, punctuation, or writing perfect sentences. Just get your ideas down on paper. Polish your first draft later.

Try It Out

Use the notes to write the first draft of a report. You do not have to use all the notes. Write on your own paper.

TOPIC: Sitting Bull
    —leader of Native American nation called the Sioux
    —upset because many settlers coming to Great Plains
    —afraid settlers would take all the food from "hunting ground"
Sitting Bull and other Native American leaders decided to fight
    —attacked wagon trains
    —fought with U.S. Army
Peace agreements didn't last
    —1868—U.S. and Sioux made peace
    —1874—General George Custer broke treaty
    —Sioux forced off land
Sitting Bull and other leaders again decided to fight
    —1876—"Custer's Last Stand"—Sioux victory—Custer killed
    —U.S. sent large army to overpower Sioux
    —Sitting Bull escaped to Canada

What Have I Learned?

Suppose you had to write a report on how to do or make something. Choose a specific example as a topic. On your own paper, tell what the main ideas of your first two paragraphs would be.

Writing the Final Copy

Read over your first draft carefully. Make corrections and changes. Polish your writing until it is good enough for your final copy.

Ask Yourself

How can you improve a first draft? Read the paragraphs. Then answer the questions.

> The Emperor and the Kite is a folktale that takes place in ancient china. The story is about the princess Djeow Seow. She is the emperor's youngest daughter. Djeow Seow is so small that her father pays almost no attention to her. It's a shame.
>
> One day, the emperor is kidnapped. Djeow Seow prooves herself more loyel than the emperor's other children. She rescues her father and wins his respect. A person's size is something the emperor learns that it has nothing to do with her worth.

1. What punctuation is missing from the first sentence? What capital letter?
   _____

2. What sentence would you take out of the first paragraph?
   _____
   _____

3. What are the two spelling mistakes in the second paragraph?
   _____

4. Rewrite the last sentence to make it clearer.
   _____
   _____

26

How To

Turn Your First Draft into the Final Copy

Read your work paragraph-by-paragraph, but read it as a whole, too. How does it sound to you? Have you accomplished your goal? Use this checklist to proofread and polish your writing:

- Have I expressed my ideas clearly?
- Have I developed each main idea with facts and details?
- Do all paragraphs relate to the topic?
- Are paragraphs smoothly connected? Does the writing flow well?
- Do all my sentences and paragraphs make sense?
- Are my facts, numbers, and dates correct?
- Do all sentences start with a capital letter and end with the correct punctuation?
- Did I use commas, quotation marks, and apostrophes correctly?
- Did I check the spelling of difficult words in a dictionary?
- Did I capitalize proper nouns?

Try It Out

The following paragraph is from the first draft of a report. Make changes and corrections until you feel it is good enough to be the final copy. Use the checklist in the **How To** box for help. Write the final version on your own paper.

> There are many alphabet systems used all over the world. Some, such as our Roman alphbet, are used by hundreds of millions of people to write dozens of different languages. others, such as the Cambodian alphabet, are used by only the people of one small country to write one or two languages. Some languages do not use alphabets at all. Alphabets are symbols that each stand for a sound. Languages like Chinese use "word pictures" that show a symbol of an entire word or idea. The Cyrillic, or Russian, alphabet is another example of an alphabet that is used to write many languages.

What Have I Learned?

Choose four questions in the **How To** box that you think are most important. Write them on your own paper, and give reasons for your choices.

LESSON 12 Making Your Writing Come Alive

Make first drafts and final copies as interesting and lively as they can be. Choose your words carefully and be creative so your writing will come alive.

Ask Yourself

What makes writing come alive? Read the two paragraphs. Then answer the questions.

Paragraph A

I slid off the chair lift onto the slope. I was high up, and it was very cold. "I should never have come skiing," I thought.

Paragraph B

As I slid off the chair lift onto the snowy slope, my blood nearly turned to ice. Not only was I looking down 3,000 feet, but it was cold enough to freeze fire. "Whose nutty idea was this?" I asked myself.

1. Which paragraph did you enjoy reading more? Explain why.
   _____
   _____

2. What details does Paragraph B contain that Paragraph A doesn't?
   _____
   _____

3. In which paragraph do sentences begin in a more interesting way? Explain.
   _____

4. Which paragraph makes you feel more as though you are there? Why?
   _____
   _____

28

How To

Make Your Writing Come Alive

- Use exact words and details. "Five thousand teenagers lined up for the rock concert" is clearer than "Many people came to the concert."
- Use figures of speech. "Sharp as a needle" is livelier than "very sharp."
- Use details that relate to the five senses. For example, "the ocean's cold, crashing waves" appeals to the senses of touch and hearing.
- Write different kinds of sentences—some short, some long.
- Don't begin too many sentences in the same way.
- Don't repeat words or ideas if you can avoid doing so.

Try It Out

Read the first draft of the composition below. Then use the **How To** suggestions to help you rewrite it to make it come alive. Use a separate sheet of paper.

> I was still half a mile from home when it began to rain. One minute it was just drizzling. Then all of a sudden it was raining very hard. I ran. The rain came down even faster. I ran faster. I was getting very wet.
>
> By the time I came around the last corner, I was soaked. I was also starting to get cold. "It sure will feel great to get inside," I thought.
>
> I had just a little farther to go. Then, just when I thought I was safe, I slipped. I landed in a big mud puddle. I got up, covered with mud. I was not happy.
>
> Just then the sun came out. Wouldn't you know it?

What Have I Learned?

Imagine that your community is holding a penny drive to raise money for the local zoo. Give three hints to make the writing in the advertisements come alive.

29

REVIEW: Preparing Written Assignments

LESSONS 1–5

Reviewing What You Learned

Write the answer to each question.

1. To do a large assignment, should you plan to do it all in one day or divide the assignment into smaller parts?

2. When you read written directions, should you pay attention only to verbs or read every word?

3. What is the first step in planning a written assignment?

4. When you do a written assignment, why should you leave space between words?

Using What You Know

Felicia had this writing assignment: "Which make better pets—dogs or cats? Write a paragraph giving your opinion. Support your opinion with reasons and examples." Read her paragraph. Then answer the questions.

cats make better pets than dogs. I have a cat named Kipper. She is gray and white and weighs about eight pounds. I wood never trade her for a dog.

1. How well did Felicia follow instructions? Explain your answer.

2. How could Felicia have made her paper neater?

3. What two corrections should Felicia make when she proofreads her work?

30

Preparing Large Written Assignments

LESSONS 6–12

Reviewing What You Learned

Write the word or phrase that best completes each sentence.

1. If you do not completely understand an assignment, ask _____ for help.

2. "The History of Asia" would not be a good topic for a one-page report because it is too _____.

3. One thing you should <u>not</u> do when you take notes is write only in _____ sentences.

4. When you organize information for a written assignment, it is important to support each main idea with _____ or _____.

5. When writing a first draft, you should not worry about making _____.

6. To make your writing come alive, use exact words and _____.

Using What You Know

Suppose your teacher gave you the writing assignment described below, due in two weeks. Answer the questions that follow.

> The United States has changed in many ways since 1900. Describe one way the country has changed. Explain why the change happened. Then tell whether you think the change was a good one. Support your opinion with clear reasons. Write three or four paragraphs.

1. How would you plan ahead to do the assignment?

_____

_____

31

2. How would you decide on a topic?

3. Suppose you decided to write about how people once traveled by horse and wagon but now travel by car. How would you organize your ideas and supporting facts and details into paragraphs?

4. Name four tips for preparing a neat, well-organized paper. For hints, refer to the **How To** boxes in this book.

5. Pretend this is the first draft of your last paragraph. Rewrite the paragraph so it is carefully worded and interesting to read.

   The use of cars has been a mighty bad change. They pollute the air, make noise, cost millions of lives in accidents. They cause trees to be cut down to make room for ugly dirty highways.